The 33% Revolution

How to End the IRS and Create A Fair and Equitable Tax System

-----------------o---------------

Respectfully submitted for your serious consideration by…

A Citizen

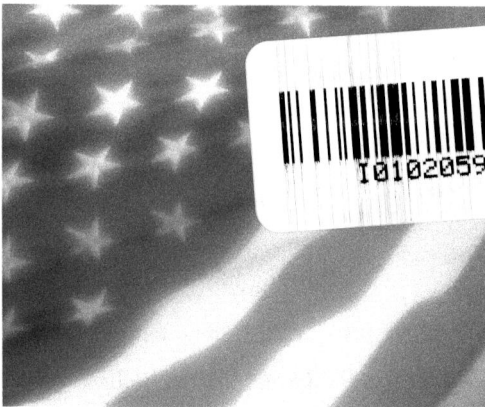

July 4, 2007, 2008, 2009, 2010, 2011, 2012, 2013, 2014, 2015, 2016, 2017, 2018, 2019

The 33% Revolution

Poor Richard Publishing Co. Denver, CO

By Jeffrey Reeves, BA, MA, EUREKONOMIST™

with Dr Agon Fly

For information, contact Poor Richard Publishing

1270 Jasmine St., Denver CO 80220

(303)355-0550 – JEFFREY.REEVES@USA.NET

Published by Poor Richard Publishing Co.

Printed in the United States of America

1st Printing July 4, 2019

Author: Jeffrey Reeves, BA, MA, Eurekonomist™ with Dr Agon Fly
Graphic Design: Sandra Reeves of Poor Richard Publishing Co.
Caricature: Robert Bauer of www.goofyfaces.com

This publication is designed to provide accurate and informative information with regard to the subject matter covered. It is sold with the understanding that the publisher is not engaged in rendering legal, accounting, or other professional advice. If legal advice or other expert assistance is required, the services of a competent professional person should be sought.

— From a Declaration of Principles jointly adopted by a Committee of the American Bar Association and a Committee of Publishers and Associations

For bulk purchases or more information please call

1-303-355-0550

Email - jeffrey.reeves@usa.net

Dedication...

I dedicate this treatise with heartfelt thanks to Benjamin Franklin, George Washington, James Madison, Thomas Jefferson, John Adams, and all our Founding Fathers and the often unnamed and unrecognized Women that stood with them and to their contemporary counterparts leading the second non-violent American Revolution through the Article V – Convention of States movement.

These men and women and many of their lesser known contemporaries and patriotic successors, although they did not agree on every item and issue that they faced in the following decades, pledged "to each other our Lives, our Fortunes, and our sacred Honor."[1]

---

[1] The final words of the Declaration of Independence.

• Table of Contents...

- o Can the Typical American Help Their Candidate or Political Party with Money...
- o Rules for Political Parties and Other Organizations...
- o Organizations Such as Labor Unions or Lobbyists...
- o Free Speech...
- **HEALTH CARE...**
  - o The Dilemma...
  - o Don't Mess with Medicare...
  - o There Is a Solution...
- **CONCLUSION** – Only you can make it happen

Introduction

"$16,427,300,000,0 00.00

Sixteen trillion, four-hundred twenty-seven billion, three-hundred million dollars...and more

This statistic shows the total personal income in the United States...for 2017. The data are in current U.S. dollars not adjusted for inflation or deflation. According to the Bureau of Economic Analysis—BEA—personal income is the income that is received by persons from all sources. It is calculated as the sum of wage and salary disbursements, supplements to wages and salaries, proprietors' income with inventory valuation and capital consumption adjustments, rental income of persons with capital consumption adjustment, personal dividend income, personal interest income, and personal current transfer receipts, less contributions for government social insurance. Personal income increased to about 16.4 trillion U.S. dollars in 2017." [2]

Now, you'd think with $16.4 trillion of potentially taxable income the Federal Government would be able to glean $4.4 trillion to satisfy its needs without incurring a deficit...but no...the best guess—and it's only a guess—by the Dolts in DC is that the government will take in *only* $3.422 trillion thru September 30, 2019.[3]

With a problem as intractable as the national debt, you'd think some brilliant bureaucrat would suggest a common-sense solution.

---

[2] Statistics derived from the US Government Bureau of Economic Analysis -
http://www.bea.gov/iTable/iTable.cfm?reqid=9&step=3&isuri=1&910=x&911=0&903=58&904=1990&905=1000&906=a#reqid=9&step=3&isuri=1&904=1990&903=58&906=a&905=1000&910=x&911=0
[3] ONLY—boy, our perception of what it takes to run the country is out of sync with most Citizens idea of costs...source of data is
https://www.thebalance.com/u-s-federal-budget-breakdown-3305789

You'd think that someone might...but obviously, no one has; or at least no one in the government has.

That's not a surprise. No one in the governmental universe wants to solve the problem. The bureaucrats thrive on playing the underfunded card and using a manipulative accounting process to guarantee more money next year regardless of need. The politicians—regardless of party or ideology—*live by promises made to get elected, not by promises kept.*

The success of both the Citizens and government of the United STATES of America *that the Founders designed to serve the states and their Citizens* was of the utmost importance to the founders. I believe the Founders would be utterly disgraced by...

- Political parties supported and controlled by insider scavengers who have access to the halls of Congress and the Lincoln Bedroom at the White House and who devour the hard-won character, principles, property, and wealth of the

Citizens of the United Sates to serve their own interests
- self-serving Congressmen and Senators....like Harry Reed...that burden American Citizens and small businesses with today's tax, education, health-care, and political systems and...in the same moment...use their office and position to enhance their personal wealth
- a court system that discounts the *principles* laid down in the U S Constitution in favor of the personal ideology and the ever changing and opportunistic *values* of Progressive judges
- an ideological executive branch ruled by shadowy insiders

The powerful in the world of bureaucrats and politicians are motivated and manipulated by the power and money they derive from the BIGS:
- Billionaire campaign contributors and PACs
- Financial entities...banks, investment businesses, insurance companies
- Lobbyists like Big Pharma and Big Ag

- Special interest groups like the environmentalists masquerading as well-meaning non-profit NGOs
- Self-serving unions like the NEA and its underlings at the state level
- Big businesses like Google, Facebook, telecom companies, public utilities...themselves pseudo governments
- Media that no longer report the news but make it up to suit themselves and the ideology they embrace

Where do you guess the legislative branch—Congress—and executive branch—President and Cabinet Secretaries—hide the rules that govern their concessions to their own and the BIGS' behavior?

If you guessed in the tax code and its thousands of pages of exemptions and in the myriad regulations propagated by bureaucrats in the executive branch interpreting legislation that comes from the Congress...you would be correct.

It doesn't have to be that way. However, the politicians, bureaucrats, and BIGS in the Hydra[4] Cartel[5] headed by the current fractured federal and state government structures[6] will never address the core issues that fail the states and virtually enslave their Citizens. It's going to take the Citizens from all fifty states to defeat the many heads of the Hydra Cartel. It's going to take a revolution.

The 33% Revolution offers the Citizens of the United States of America a way to non-violently lop off the heads of the Hydra Cartel...a way never before possible...a way that every demographic that is not a part of the Hydra Cartel can contribute to with time, talent, and treasure.

Read on and you will be encouraged, maybe enthused, hopefully motivated, ready to be a voice for millions of Citizens, and armed with the golden sword of social media and crowd sourcing.

---

[4] https://en.wikipedia.org/wiki/Lernaean_Hydra
[5] https://www.merriam-webster.com/dictionary/cartel
[6] Structures such as civil service systems, education systems, election systems, legislative systems, and especially the tax systems.

FIRST, LET'S AGREE...

W ould you agree that...

- The IRS has nearly a hundred-thousand of pages of regulations.

   The words on those pages don't help you live a better life. You don't need that.

- Every year between January 1st and April 15th you have to collect a bunch of records in a shoebox so someone can prepare your taxes; or, you have to take a lot of time out of your life to fill out pages and pages of forms to file your taxes yourself. This puts a lot of stress on you or takes money out of your pocket or both.

> *You don't need more stress and less money.*

- When members of Congress leave office and Cabinet appointees quit working for the President, they often find jobs as lobbyists with special interest groups, big labor, and big business. Then they wander around Washington DC telling elected and appointed officials how to write tax laws. They eat in fancy restaurants and take expensive junkets.

> *They don't help you in any way.*

- Corrupt and dishonest 527's and other groups that want to promote some half-baked idea spend hundreds-of-millions of dollars to elect their puppets to Congress and state legislative bodies. These elected lawmakers get their money under the table from rich people who want to control America's politics and manipulate America's economy.

> *You don't need a narrowly focused special interest group, or a 527 political action group funded by a wealthy businessperson, a corrupt union boss, misguided special interest group, or misinformed celebrity telling you how to think and vote.*

- America has a patchwork system of health care that Obamacare has burdened with a trillion dollars in overhead and a labyrinthine bureaucracy. It does not take care of every American and is too expensive for many families.

  You need reliable health care and affordable health insurance.
- Many Americans can't retire at all or take a big cut in pay if they do retire. The government keeps making up new "plans" to "help" people with retirement but, how secure do most of us feel about retiring comfortably?

  You need to be able to face the rest of your life with confidence that you will have enough money to live comfortably and pay for your daily and long-term needs without being a burden on your children or society.

Do you agree?
Read on...

Would you agree that instead of the current system:

- You deserve a compassionate tax system where the Citizens' Revenue Service works *for* the taxpayer and not for the politicians and the special interests...
- You deserve a tax system that makes it easy to report, pay, and file your taxes...
- You deserve a tax system that denies greedy and self-interested lobbyists access to the halls of government...
- You deserve a tax system that supports the federal election process financially and in a significant way so that the character and policy ideas of the candidates are what America sees, not just the drivel disguised as news by the pundits, the cardboard cartoon-like images of candidates that 527's create,

and the talking points consultants contrive...

- You deserve a national system of health care that makes sure you can go to the doctor when you need to without wondering if you can afford it...
- You deserve retirement options that allow you to retire with dignity and without worrying about being a burden when you are living the last years of your life...

Is a tax system like that possible? Not under the current system where taxes are the plaything of politicians and lobbyists but a burden on you.

Is there anything you can do? Yes! *The 33 % Revolution solves these problems for you and takes taxes out of the hands of the politicians and lobbyists. Contact your Congressperson and Senators and tell them you want the 33% Revolution enacted as law right away.*[7]

---

[7] Of course, the people in power will resist just like the British resisted The Founding Fathers and the Declaration of Independence. Fear not. If you persist, you will prevail.

What's the solution?

Change the paradigm.

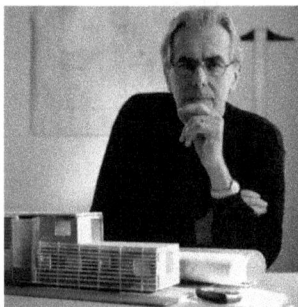

The tax system[8], for many decades, has promoted the agenda of the few – presidents and congress, big business, big labor, special interest groups, and trade associations - at the expense of "We the people..." – the 300 million+ Citizens of the United States of America. The tax system has turned into a monster and not even all 300 million of us can *change* it, *but* we can kill the monster and force Congress to start all over again.

The politicians and special interests that are currently benefiting from the system will <u>never</u> change it or consider killing it unless and until you and millions of other Americans demand it.

---

[8] The tax system includes dozens if not hundreds of separate and individual taxes on everything from tobacco to alcohol to gasoline to telephone service and so on. They all must go.

The current income tax system is the goose that lays the golden eggs for politicians and lobbyists.

Hear this loud and clear: **the current tax system is the Golden Goose for the few; not for America Citizens; not for you; and you do not get any of the golden eggs.**

The ONLY way to get rid of the current system is for 100 million Americans to *demand* that Congress scrap the old system and start all over.

The current system feeds elected officials and the lobbyists very well. It puts money into presidential, senate and house election campaigns through the lobbyists and money in the till of the lobbyists through legislation and the awarding of government contracts by the executive branch.

The only way to rid America of this broken system is to kill the monster it has become and create a better system.

Only commonsensible Americans who accept the challenge to create an entirely new system of taxation can do this. It will take *millions* of Americans to make a difference.

Anthropologist Margaret Mead:

"Never doubt that a small group of thoughtful, committed Citizens can change the world.

Indeed, it is the only thing that ever has."

"What's in it for me?" you ask.

"Life, liberty and the pursuit of happiness" and if that isn't enough, you'll be a part of the 21st Century revolution that returns power to "We the people..."

The 33% Revolution...

The 33% Revolution is one such system.

The 33% Revolution is based on common sense ideas that every working American, self employed person, small business owner, corporate executive and government employee can easily understand and agree with – at least they will if they are honest and not looking out only for themselves.

At the same time, you can bet that those who suck the golden eggs out of the current system will find dozens of arguments against any approach that

- denies them the booty that they snatch from the system that they have created and corrupted to serve themselves
- unburdens you and every other American from excessive taxes and reporting requirements

In fact, those who serve in government receive many benefits that elude all but the wealthiest Citizens.

The 33% Revolution believes that all Citizens, regardless of who their employer is, should receive the same treatment.

Therefore, *The 33% Revolution* thinks that all existing government benefit programs should be ended and the people who serve us in the legislative, executive, and judicial branches of government, whether elected, appointed, or hired, should equally participate in *The 33% Revolution.* [9]

---

[9] The obvious argument against this lies in the reality that taxes paid by government employers on behalf of their employees are being taken from one pocket and put into another of the same pair of pants. However, not requiring the same accounting rules for the government could lead to all kinds of mischief.
The same things happen in state and local government. States that adopt a system comparable to *The 33% Revolution* could solve these same problems at the state and local levels. Perhaps the Federal legislation that creates *The 33% Revolution* should include incentives for the states to do so.

The Basics...

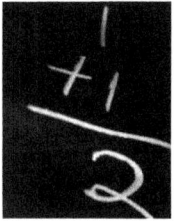

The basic premise of *The 33% Revolution* is this; if 33% of every Americans' income is paid *by their employer* to the federal government as a tax, the federal government will have plenty of money to take care of all of us in peace and in war, in sickness and in health, till death do us part.[10]

- Americans deserve a compassionate tax system where the administrators work for the taxpayer and not visa versa
    The 33% Revolution is fair and compassionate.
- Americans deserve a tax system that minimizes and simplifies reporting, paying and filing taxes
    The 33% Revolution minimizes and, in most cases, eliminates the

---

[10] Anyone who would like to back-test this thesis could go back to 1974 when this idea first developed in almost the exact form presented in this essay. They would discover that *The 33% Revolution* would have generated adequate governmental income to pay all the bills and leave enough in the kitty to handle the challenges of the national debt, Social Security, and health care that America faces today.

need for individuals to file a tax return.

- Americans deserve a tax system that is free from the excessive influence on legislation and the awarding of contracts by greedy and self-interested lobbyists
  The 33% Revolution makes lobbying obsolete in its current form.

- Americans deserve a tax system that supports the federal election process financially and in a significant way. The aim here is to make sure that the character and policy ideas of the candidates are what American Citizens see, not just the cardboard cartoon-like images of candidates that 527's create, the media drivel disguised as news, and the talking points consultants make up.
  The 33% Revolution entirely removes special interests from the election process.

- Americans deserve a national funding system for health care that makes sure every American can afford health insurance
  The 33% Revolution preserves Medicare and guarantees health care to all Americans.

- Americans deserve retirement options that allow them to retire with dignity and without worrying about taxes when they are living the last years of their lives.

The 33% Revolution makes retirement income planning a simple tax-neutral process that benefits every American.

Now, before you go screaming into the night that such a tax is unfair to the little guy – that would be you and me – or to the small business owner, read the next section.

THE INCOME TAX...

The Graduated Scale...

The maximum amount of the tax that individuals would pay out of their own pocket would be based on a graduated scale. Employers could choose to pay both the employer percentage and the employee percentage. Here's how that works.[11]

If you earn	you pay	your employer pays
$0 to $10,000	1%	32%
$10,001 to $20,000	2	31
$20,001 to $30,000	3	30
$30,001 to $40,000	4	29
$40,001 to $50,000	5	28
$50,001 to $60,000	6	27
$60,001 to $70,000	7	26
$70,001 to $80,000	8	25
$80,001 to $90,000	9	24
$90,001 to $100,000	10	23
and so on until income reaches $320,000		
$320,001 or more	33%	0%[12]

---

[11] Of course, the scale used here is for illustration only. The actual earnings scale would be based on research conducted at the time the law is passed.

[12] The "earned income" schedule would be adjusted for inflation. The tax rates could be reduced if the government's income exceeds expense but could not be adjusted up except in time of national emergency. See the entire schedule in Attachment A.

An important question in *The 33% Revolution* is, "What is considered earned income?"

Business owners and executives often receive benefits that ordinary employees do not receive. *The 33% Revolution* defines "earned income" this way: anything of value that an employee receives or uses is "earned income"...commissions, bonuses, a company car, stock options, a vacation, spousal travel on business trips, free meals, group insurance benefits, etc[13].

"Income" refers only to "earned income" not to income on savings and investments. *The 33% Revolution* allows the individual taxpayer to pay taxes on the growth and income they earn from savings and investments either
- in the year in which they are earned or
- as an estate tax at the death of the taxpayer (see the Estate Tax section below[14])

The Citizens' Revenue Service would receive the same kind of income reporting from investment firms that it currently receives in order to keep track of this kind of income.

---

[13] The Citizens' Revenue Service can come up with a list that is much more comprehensive but creates the desired result.
[14] Taxpayers who choose to pay the taxes when they receive unearned income can effectively eliminate the need to have their heirs pay any estate tax after their death but may, in fact, pay more tax than is needed.

What About Business Expenses?

An employee or business owner that uses a company car as an essential part of a job - for example a service tech or an outside salesperson – would not pay tax on the expenses the company reimburses. On the other hand, an employee cannot automatically exclude from income every dollar s/he might call a business expense. The Citizens' Revenue Service would have to make rules for employers to follow that would be fair to employees, small business owners, employers and the rest of Americans.

Who Pays the Taxes and Who Must Report to the Citizens' Revenue Service?

Employers calculate, report and pay all the taxes for employees.[15] You do not have to file income tax returns if you are an hourly or salaried or commission income employee. Your employer will send you a statement of earnings at the end of each year, but you do not need to file any kind of return under normal circumstances.

---

[15] Contract employees that work for more than one employer would have to file a consolidated statement of earnings. They would include the entire 33% tax in their billing rate to their clients and would file returns as business owners.

Companies, therefore, pay the taxes and are responsible for reporting both the taxes and the income paid to each employee to the Citizens' Revenue Service. This income reporting is very important because it may affect taxes due during retirement and at your death. A big part of the Citizens' Revenue Service's job will be to make sure employers are reporting and paying all the taxes. Individual Citizens will never be held responsible for paying taxes. If an employer fails to pay taxes due on your income, it will not affect your retirement income or estate taxes.

Do Companies Pay Taxes?

The tax money companies pay to the Citizens' Revenue Service on your income is the company's tax burden. In other words, American companies pay taxes based on the labor that goes into the production of their products and services instead of paying a corporate income tax. In both the long run and the short term, this creates more revenue for the government and employers pay higher taxes only on the earned income of the employees.

However, the reduced staff costs for accounting and tax preparation should partially offset the tax expense to employers. More importantly, this approach lets businesses focus on doing the business they are chartered to do. Businesses—especially small businesses—don't have to spend time and energy struggling through a mile-high set of rules to manage and minimize their tax burden.

Employees also benefit because their companies will be able to measure and reward individual and group productivity without having material costs adversely affecting the performance of the employees.

Why Is That Important?

Since there are no special tax considerations given to individual companies or to specific industries, businesses no longer have a reason to send lobbyists to Washington DC to promote some tax scheme that benefits just one company or just one industry. (Knowing the character of our Executive and the Congress in recent years and the greed of the tax lobbyists, it won't be long until they find new ways of manipulating the system to their own advantage. As Goldie Hawn's character in the movie *Protocol* said, you'll need to watch them "...like a hawk..."

Doesn't That Put an Extra Burden on Small Businesses?

The self-employed, small business owners, independent contractors, real estate investors, and professional practices (like accountants, attorneys, doctors and any other business where the owners rely on profits and may not receive salaries or wages) would have to file tax returns just like other businesses. They would pay the employer portion of taxes for their employees but would only have to pay the employee portion on their own earnings.[16]

The wisdom of this may escape some who think all small businesses make a ton of money. Remember that you must include moms that provide child-care in their homes, the local handyman, plumber, electrician, and yard-care person. You must also consider that the more highly compensated professionals – doctors, accountants, attorneys, architects, etc. - will still be paying a lot of money in taxes...in many cases they'll pay the full 33%.

---

[16] Here again, the Citizens' Revenue Service would need to develop a set of rules to make sure that greedy business owners would not take advantage by hiding money that was "earned income" in the business.

What About Non-profits Like the Red Cross and AARP?

Non-profits that are recognized *charities* or that provide services to the general population would be exempt from paying the employer portion of the taxes. Non-profits like AARP and those that serve special interest groups like labor unions, trade associations, ethnic groups or racially based organizations could pay a reduced percentage of the employer portion as long as they could demonstrate that
- they were providing services to their constituents and to the general public that were not available elsewhere.
- they were not actively promoting a political or ideological point of view
- they were not selling products to generate revenue to support their agenda[17]

Political parties, 527's (if *The 33% Revolution* doesn't rid America of this scourge) and similar organizations would have to pay the full employer contribution since they specifically promote ideological and political agendas. [18]

---

[17] Organizations such as Goodwill might be exempt since their business is creating jobs by selling recycled products.
[18] One approach to this entire situation is to have a graduated scale for non-profits where the non-profit would qualify for a

Does the Federal Government Support Business?

There are, of course, issues that are greater than taxes. It might make sense for the Federal Government to support, for example, research that would free us from dependence on foreign oil, find a cure for cancer, or preserve endangered species. The Federal Government could do this through legislation in Congress, and by executive decisions when awarding contracts to companies or non-profits that are involved in research and development that addresses identified national needs. (Remember to watch them "...like a hawk...")

What About Foreign Companies That Import Goods to the USA?

Under *The 33% Revolution,* foreign companies that import goods into America – whether parts to be assembled here or finished goods – would pay an import tax that would put the labor cost in the price of their goods on parity with labor costs in America. This protects

---

1/3rd or 2/3rd reduction in their tax burden based on the status they receive from the Citizens' Revenue Service. Therefore, the Red Cross might be considered a full non-profit and pay no matching tax while Planned Parenthood might receive only a 1/3rd reduction in its taxes and the 527's would receive none.

American workers without being unfair to workers in other countries.[19]

What Else Will the Citizens' Revenue Service Do?

The 33% Revolution replaces the IRS with the Citizens' Revenue Service whose main job is to oversee tax reporting and collection. In addition, since companies - not individuals – pay all the taxes, this approach simplifies the collection process and would save billions of dollars every year.

Local government (city, township, county, etc.) could collect the Federal Tax and charge a fee to the IRS for doing so. Since most local governments already collect taxes and track employment, they could keep a close watch on the employers within their boundaries and the Citizens' Revenue Service could support their efforts and oversee their activity. When a local government does not have an income tax of its own, the County or State Government could collect the taxes for them.

---

[19] Import taxes are complex and have both economic and diplomatic impact. The Citizens' Revenue Service and the various Federal Government Agencies that deal with this issue will need to co-ordinate their regulations and practices to make this work. Many believe that interagency co-operation among federal bureaucracies is impossible but A. Citizen isn't one of them.

In any case, the local, county, or state government would deposit the money collected in a local bank—not a national too-big-to-fail mega-bank—for up to 90 days. This would allow the money to serve the local community before forwarding it to the Citizens' Revenue Service. Considering the events of late summer and early autumn 2008, this approach seems ever more appealing.

RETIREMENT AND ESTATE TAXES...

Social Security...

When Social Security was initially enacted in 1935 it was intended to provide working Americans with a base retirement income from the Social Security System. This is still a valid aim for the Social Security System. The question is not *whether The 33% Revolution* will provide this base income. It must. The question is *how The 33% Revolution* directs the government to manage the money to insure this benefit.

The 33% Revolution addresses this question from a unique perspective. If America wants a Social Security System that does what it was intended to do, then America must face up to the fact that the Social Security System designed in 1935 is not good enough to serve the retirees of 2035 and beyond. We aren't driving cars designed in 1935 or putting 1935 appliances in our homes. Why in the world are we relying on an outdated Social Security

System that was designed in 1935 and hasn't been substantially changed since?

The 33% Revolution believes it may take a temporary surtax on employers to fund the Social Security System through a transition period and a Restructured Social Security System to guarantee the income of future retirees. [20]

Spineless and greedy politicians in Washington DC refuse to consider any change to the Social Security System because they fear
- accountability for their spending
- having to present America with a balanced budget
- the reaction of powerful lobbyists who rely on scaring the hell out of senior Citizens in order to sell them more products

Americans are not stupid. If an alternative approach looks reasonable and gives back as much - or more - than it takes away, Americans will embrace it.

[20] A. Citizen does not have time or money to study this issue in detail, but the Congress wastes enough money every year to protect the failing (if not already failed) Social Security System that it is certain they could come up with a couple of million to research some alternatives. They might take a page out of the book of the more successful *mutual* insurance companies that have delivered *guaranteed* retirement income to policy owners for almost 200 years.

Lobbyist organizations like AARP, that act more in their own interest than in the interest of those they claim to serve, throw up a smoke screen of scare tactics whenever a new idea comes along...especially if it would reduce their assumed-but-not-deserved power over the aforementioned Congress. As American Citizens, we need to rid ourselves of as much lobbyist influence in the Congress of the United States as we can...especially when it comes to Social Security. If we don't, there will never be clear thinking on this (or any other) subject the congress addresses.

Retirement Income and Estate Taxes in *The 33% Revolution*?

American's who retire should not have to bear the same tax burden as those who are still working. That does not mean that they should be exempt from paying taxes. *The 33% Revolution* is used as the income tax schedule and a combined retirement/estate tax schedule. Once a person elects to "retire",[21]

---

[21] "Retire" means that you choose – at any age – to remove yourself from the "earned income" tax system and enter the "retirement/estate tax" system. It has nothing to do with age. It depends entirely on the choice of the individual to quite

the Citizens' Revenue Service exempts that person's *unearned* income[22] from taxation until "retirement income" exceeds that person's pre-retirement "earned income" that was already taxed.

The Citizens' Revenue Service will know – just as the current IRS knows - exactly how much you earn in a lifetime. You will have already paid tax on that amount. Therefore, when you (or the second spouse in the case of married couples) "retire" or die, any asset you still own or control that adds up to less than the amount the Citizens' Revenue Service shows you had earned during your working years will not be taxed.

For example, assume that you made $1 million during your working career. You wisely saved some money and invested carefully. The mortgage on your $200,000.00 home is paid off when you "retire." Your savings and investments have grown to $1 million and you only take interest and earnings from these accounts at the rate of $50,000.00 per year.

---

working for wages and to live off accumulated assets. The taxpayer can do this at any time, but it will not make sense to do so at an early age or if the taxpayer is still employed. A. Citizen feels certain that financial planners and advisors will become invaluable to folks who contemplate early "retirement."

[22] Obviously, if you are still working for wages or engaged in your own business, you are not "retired".

This leaves the $1 million you saved intact. When you die, 20 years later, you will have taken $1 million of income from your retirement funds ($50,000.00 per year time twenty years). That money was tax-free because it didn't exceed the $1 million you had earned during your working career.

This means your estate - the $1 million you had invested and your home, which is now valued at about $400,000.00, is worth $1.4 million. Your heirs would pay the 33% Retirement/estate Tax and receive about $1 million from you as a legacy.

What if You Give a Gift to a Charity?

Gifts to recognized *charities*[23] after retirement would reduce the size of your estate and therefore the taxes that your estate would have to pay. If you make a charitable gift while you are still paying "earned income" taxes, you can report that gift in the year it is made and receive a tax credit for taxes you would have paid on an income amount equal to the value of gift.

You can make personal gifts whenever you wish up to $12,000 per year per giver and per

---

[23] The Citizens' Revenue Service will define "charities" to exclude the types of organizations referenced above.

recipient.[24] That means, for example, that you and your spouse could give each of your children and each of your grandchildren $24,000 each year and it would have no effect on your "earned income" taxes.[25] It would add to the estate and incomes of the beneficiaries and reduce your taxable estate that exceeded your "earned income" retirement/estate tax exemption.

The gift tax process that *The 33% Revolution* advocates is similar to the gift tax program of the current system. It is one of the better parts of that system.

Where Does That Leave Pensions, 401(k)'s, etc?

Pensions, 401(k)'s, and the myriad of other retirement schemes that plague American workers and employers are the result of decades of lobbying for "tax-favored" retirement plans. When you look at all of these programs closely, it is apparent that "the system" created them and they would not be needed when *The 33% Revolution* replaced the mile-high tax code.

---

[24] The $12,000 amount is arbitrary, could be different, and would be adjusted annually for inflation.
[25] You could also give $12,000 each – or $24,000 – to anyone else you might want to regardless of your relationship to that person.

Tax-amnesty for American Workers' Money.

The money that these programs currently hold belongs to you and to other individual Americans who put their hard-earned dollars into them. There is no reason why you should not receive your money back with no strings attached, no penalties, tax-free. You could then put your money into any money buckets you choose – insurance, annuities, mutual funds, real estate, a tin can in the back yard – and take it out when you want. This money would become a part of your estate and would be treated the same as other retirement income and estate assets as discussed above.

Tax-amnesty for American workers' money seems like a deal that would hurt no one and would help everyone. The companies that are currently managing your money would continue to have the opportunity to do so. Your employer would be unburdened from their reporting requirements. The Citizens' Revenue Service would not have to track hundreds of thousands of "plans" but would not lose a penny since *The 33% Revolution* would produce more revenue than the old system did with all of its rules and exceptions to its rules.

New Retirement Plans From Your Employer?

If employers need to provide "retirement" benefits to attract and retain the best workers, the marketplace would dictate how they should do that. *The 33% Revolution* would tax these benefits using "earned income" rates but – and this is important – the employer would put all the money into these plans and would pay all the taxes. Employers' would be able to create longer vesting schedules than those in the current system. However, they could not keep you from taking all the money they put aside for you for longer than is reasonable.[26]

Life Insurance...

Life insurance death benefits paid to a spouse (directly or through the estate of the deceased person) and life insurance death benefits paid to a named beneficiary would be free of income tax and estate tax as they are today. These monies become a part of the estate of the beneficiary and incur a tax only at the death of the beneficiary. Proceeds payable to a trust are also tax-free and incur a 33% tax when the trust owner closes the trust or distributes money to the beneficiaries of the trust. [27]

---

[26] This is another case where the Citizens' Revenue Service would need to make some rules to protect all the parties.
[27] Life insurance death benefits payable to certain kinds of trusts will need special rules to make sure the taxpayer, the

government and the Citizenry are all treated fairly.

The Tale of a Taxpayer...

Boy John took his first job at the age of 12 mowing lawns in his neighborhood.

Each neighbor that boy John worked for paid him $15.00 per cutting. The neighbors also reported and paid the Citizens' Revenue Service the 33% tax on boy John's earnings. Boy John's neighborhood customers contributed 32% of the tax and withheld 1% from boy John's pay as his contribution. At the end of the year, they gave boy John a one-page report showing what they had paid. Boy John earned just over $1,800.00 in this first year as a taxpayer. His neighborhood customers paid a tax-deductible total of $576.00 on boy John's behalf and boy John paid $18.00.

During the next six years, young John expanded his lawn service business to include snow removal and other miscellaneous caretaking services. Young John earned nearly $9,000.00 in his senior year in high school. His neighborhood customers continued to pay the 33% tax on the wages they paid to young John. Since his earnings were still under $10,000.00 the neighborhood customers contributed and paid 32% of the tax [$2,880.00], which they deducted from their own income, and paid young John's 1% [$90.00], which the neighborhood customers withheld from young John's pay.

During his college years, young man John expanded his yard care business further. Since he now had equipment to buy and maintain he no longer worked directly for his customers but formed a company and billed his customers. That meant that his neighborhood customers would not have to pay young man John's taxes. During the four summers of his college career young man John's company earned about $36,000.00 each year. After expenses, young man John was able to clear about $18,000.00 for himself. Since young man John was now employed by his company and earned between $10,000.00 and $19,999.99, the company paid 31% of the taxes due and John paid 2% tax on his net income - a total of $5,940.00. John cleared $12,060.00 for himself.

After John graduated from college at age 22, he took an accounting internship with a CPA firm at a salary of $27,000.00 and with a promise that once he passed his CPA exam's he would receive a promotion and a raise. Since John was now employed full-time, he could not maintain his yard care business, so he sold it to a larger company for $24,000.00 and paid the Citizens' Revenue Service 33% of the sale price - $7,920.00 as an income tax. John added the remaining $16,080.00 to the $7,920.00 that he held in a private savings/investment program that his parents helped him set up when he was 12 for a total of $24,000.00. Because John was not "earning" the interest and growth on this account with his labor, it is not "earned" income and is not taxed as earned. (More about this later.)

During his internship, John received monthly paychecks of $2,250.00 from his employer. Because John's earnings were between

$20,000.00 and $29,999.99, the employer paid 30% of John's 33% tax each month - $675.00 - and withheld 3% from John's paycheck - $67.50.

When John earned his CPA, the firm promoted him and raised his salary to $36,000.00 per year - $3,000.00 each month. Since this moved John, CPA into the next bracket - $30,000 to $39,999.99 – John CPA paid 4% of his income in tax and the firm paid 29%. And so it went for the next 40 years or so. John CPA ultimately became Partner John, earning well over the top bracket of $320,000.00 per year and paid the 33% tax out of his own earnings.

Over John's 50-year employment career – age 12 to age 62 – he had earned a total of $6,300,000.00. John and his employers paid the taxes on this earned income. Since John had been Ben Franklin frugal throughout his life, he had also amassed a nice estate of equity in his home ($1,000,000.00) savings ($2,000,000.00) and investments ($4,000,000.00).

Unfortunately, for the sake of this story, we allow John to die at this time in order to illustrate how his estate would be taxed. John created an estate of $7,000,000.00 during his lifetime, which passed to his wife, Mary, free of taxes. Assuming Mary...

- used only the tax-free income from the estate for her personal income and maintenance
- the value of the estate didn't grow
- she didn't gift any of the estate away

when Mary dies the estate will be taxed on the difference between what John earned and paid taxes on during his lifetime and the total value of the estate at Mary's death.

John earned and paid taxes on $6,300,000.00 during his life and left an estate of $7,000,000.00 at his wife Mary's death. (Excuse the chauvinism. Mary could have just as easily been the breadwinner, but I had to make a decision. Besides, I had to kill John and Mary got to survive.) Therefore, the difference of $700,000.00 would, be subject to taxation at the same 33% rate. The estate would pay a tax of $231,000.00 allowing the heirs to receive $6,769,000.00 in accordance with John and Mary's wishes.

If we were to suppose that John and Mary had only one child, Emily, and she inherited the entire estate, then Emily would have to pay the 33% tax on the $6,769,000.00 at her death insofar as it was more than her earnings during her lifetime.

This is not the current system. The current system is a hodge-podge of rules and regulations that takes an army of IRS Agents, tax attorneys, CPA's and just plain Americans to manage. The current system—if you can call it that—is burdensome, incomprehensible, out of control, and *needs* to be scrapped. It does not serve the country well and does not serve *"We the people…"* at all.

Read on.

BE PREPARED TO ACT!

FEDERAL ELECTIONS...

Paying for Campaigns...

> "Though no one can go back and make a
> brand-new start, anyone can start from
> now and make a brand new ending."
> Carl Bard

The 33% Revolution would provide adequate
funding to all qualifying candidates for
presidential, senate and congressional offices. [28]

The IRS would distribute these funds to all
qualifying candidates. Each qualified
candidate would receive equal amounts of
money based on formulas agreed upon within

---

[28] A separate and independent Elections Commission would
decide how candidates qualify for these funds.

each state and district and they could use this money as they saw fit for their individual campaigns.

Candidates for President, the Senate, or Congress could not raise money from any outside source other than the political party with which they are affiliated. Individual candidates would not be permitted to spend any of their personal money for campaign purposes. The Citizens' Revenue Service would distribute the funds and the Federal Election Commission would manage the process.

Can the Typical American Help Their Candidate or Political Party with Money?

Every taxpayer would, however, be allowed, and encouraged to support the process by making additional contributions to *The 33% Revolution* Election Fund.[29] Individuals could also contribute to political parties and to specific candidates through the candidate's party.

Rules for Political Parties and Other Organizations...

---

[29] You would do this by telling your employer to withhold a few extra dollars from your pay and give it to the Election Fund.

Political parties could not accept more than $1000.00 from any one person per presidential candidate, Senate seat, or Congressional seat. Only you could make these contributions; other individuals, businesses or organizations could not make these contributions on your behalf. This avoids wealthy individuals and organizations with a lot of money from having too much influence with the political parties.

Political parties could spend any amount of money for their candidates. Political parties could allocate all their money to a single candidate or they could spread it among several or all candidates. However, if you contributed to a specific candidate of a Political Party, that money would have to be used to support that candidate unless the candidate released the money to be used elsewhere.

How About Other Organizations Such as Labor Unions or Lobbyists?

Organizations must be qualified political parties *and* must have a *unique* candidate on the ballot in order to do any campaign advertising, soliciting, etc. A candidate from one political party (let's say the Martian Party) would not qualify as a candidate for another political party (let's call it the Moon Party) that wants to support that Martian Party's candidate.

If an organization like the Firefighters Union or the Free Enterprise Association wants to "endorse" a candidate and to promote and support a candidate, they may do so and they can use as much of their money as they want. They would not, however, be allowed to mention opposing candidates or political parties in their advertising or promotions.

The Federal Election Commission would have jurisdiction over the process that qualifies political parties and candidates and the creation and enforcement of rules relating to campaigns.

Free Speech...

A. Citizen recognizes that there is a "free speech" issue involved here. A. Citizen also realizes that the ranting of "independent" voices, in ideologically motivated groups, sanctioned by poorly conceived existing law destroys the integrity of the campaign process. It is important that *Americans* resolve this issue and remove these negative forces from the election process.[30]

---

[30] A. Citizen recognizes that this is a thorny issue and will likely generate a great deal of debate. However, the problem that our current election system create needs to be solved. Hopefully, the ideas in this segment will encourage discussion and debate that lead to a common sense solution.

HEALTH CARE...

A Dilemma...

"Nothing will ever be attempted, if all possible objections must first be overcome." Samuel Johnson

Health care is a particularly difficult issue for the Federal Government to deal with.

- Creating a national health plan and socializing medical care as Obamacare did and current candidates propose, takes the free enterprise system out of the equation. Removing free enterprise from such a complex issue is creating many more problems than it solves.
- Ignoring the issues that make the system less effective than it could and should be is also problematic.
- The ideas put forward here are a starting point in a discussion that needs to be focused on providing health care—not insurance—without allowing the government to control the process or the

programs needed to execute a
commonsense health care system.

Here Is One Way to Look at A Revolution...

- Allow Medicare to cover the children of
  America universally until they are 25
  years old...
    - o If a child is covered or is eligible
      for coverage under a parent's
      policy, then Medicare only covers
      what the primary plan doesn't
      cover.
    - o The State Agency would cover
      parentless children. A revenue
      sharing program between state
      and federal government, perhaps
      something like Medicaid, would pay
      for this coverage.
    - o When parents cannot cover a child
      because they do not have health
      insurance, then Medicare would be
      mandatory and primary for the
      child, but parents would have to
      contribute to the cost.
    - o The parents' contributions would
      be equal to three times their tax
      rate[31]. If the parents were in the
      10% bracket for taxes, they would

---

[31] This is an arbitrary number and would likely need thoughtful
evaluation.

pay 30% of the Medicare cost. If they were in the highest tax bracket and paying the entire 33% tax, they would then pay 100% of the Medicare cost. (A. Citizen believes a similar formula could be applied to all Medicare recipients.)

- Employers
  - Employers would not be required to make health insurance available to all employees.
  - Employers who agreed to pay a part of the premium for health insurance plans approved by the employer, would not have to pay the employer's income tax contribution on those premiums.
  - Employees would be required to pay a part of the premium. The employee contributions would be equal to three times their tax rate. If the employee were in the 10% bracket for taxes, s/he would pay 30% of the total insurance premium. If s/he were in the highest 33% tax bracket and personally paying the entire tax, s/he would then pay 100% of the premium cost.

- o Money paid for health care premiums would reduce the employees "earned income."
- Insurance companies would be required to:
  - o allow all individuals to purchase insurance regardless of their medical conditions
  - o continue to cover individuals who qualify for unemployment benefits
    - individuals would continue to pay their share of the premium based on the amount of income they receive from unemployment insurance. The state unemployment system would pay the balance.
    - If a person exhausts their unemployment benefits, cannot find work and cannot afford to continue paying for their health insurance, they will be become a temporary Medicare beneficiary and pay some portion of the premium based on their ability to do so.[32]

---

[32] Here again, the Medicare Administrators would have to develop fair and balanced rules.

- o The Federal government would establish an FDIC-like reinsurance agency, *funded by the Federal Government and insurance companies*, to reimburse insurance companies for costs they incur on any given patient that exceed a specified amount – say $100,000.00 in a year or $1,000,000.00 in a lifetime.[33] This allows insurance companies to control their costs, accept everyone regardless of their medical conditions, and still charge affordable premiums.[34] It also keeps the government out of the free enterprise health care business and system for most Americans.
- *The 33% Revolution* could include provision to impose a medical-care tax surcharge in years where expenses are greater than budgeted.

---

[33] The government could use a process called re-insurance to alleviate the strain such a system might place on the budget in some extreme situations.

[34] An actuary (that's a person who is really good with numbers and loves to study how one event or cost affects another) would determine the actual amounts that might make sense. The average American incurs less than $3,500.00 per year in medical costs but some medical treatments cost millions.

CONCLUSION...Only YOU can make it happen...

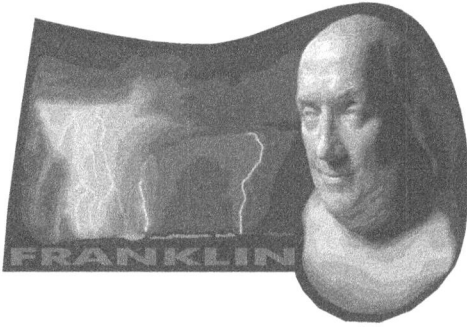

Ben Franklin wrote a treatise entitled *The Way to Wealth* in which Poor Richard Saunders outlined the wisdom of the day by reporting a talk given by "Father Abraham." He talked to a group of Citizens, just prior to an auction, about everything from savings and debt to taxes and big government. At the conclusion, Poor Richard wrote, "Thus [Father Abraham] ended his harangue. The people heard it and approved the doctrine, *and immediately practiced the contrary*..."

A. Citizen begs you, "Please, don't be like the people at that auction 250 years ago."

- The current system of taxation is broken beyond repair.

- The only way the American people – you and I – will ever escape from this monster is to kill it completely and replace it with a 21st century system that recognizes and corrects the errors of the past.
- Our elected officials *will not change the system* that keeps laying golden eggs in their nests.
- The lobbyists are too powerful. America needs to rid itself of them.
- The election process has become perverted by influence peddlers and ideologues who care only for their issues and care not about the United STATES of America
- There is no reasonable health care solution forthcoming from the Congress or the White House or any candidates for those offices...all the proposals they are parading before you are designed by money hungry special interest groups or power grabbing politicians and are not in the common interest
- Retirement planning has become a patchwork quilt of plans and programs that carry large price tags and promise only mediocre results[35]

---

[35] A recent study predicts that 90% of baby boomers will rely on the government, family, or continued work during retirement.

The 33% Revolution resolves these issues in *your* favor. *Use the system to change the system…*

Contact your Congressperson, your Senator, and the White House and tell them to adopt *The 33% Revolution.*[36]

Contact your family, friends, neighbors, co-workers, doctor, dentist…anyone you can think of… and refer them to *The 33% Revolution* web site and encourage them to buy a copy of *The 33% Revolution.*

www.33PercentRevolution.com

Tell them to contact Congress with the message:

IT'S TIME - Adopt *The 33% Revolution.*

> *"We have it in our power to begin the world over again."* Thomas Paine

If not you – who? If not now – when?

---

[36] Links to congressional email addresses in Appendix B.

We need to send MILLIONS of messages to Washington D.C. to make this happen.

Respectfully and hopefully submitted for your serious consideration...

July 4, 2019 *A.*

Citizen

PS – A. Citizen is not naïve. Even if millions of Americans demand this change, the congress will fool with it and try to reinvent their Golden Goose. A. Citizen encourages every person who reads this essay to go to www.33percentrevolution.com and add their opinions, comments and observations. A. Citizen is certain that there are dozens, hundreds, or even thousands of ideas that would improve *The 33% Revolution*. It would be best if those ideas came directly from the people and not through congress, lobbyists and their "people".

The money that you spend to buy this essay will go toward watching the folks in DC "...like a hawk..." and toward further promoting

The Revolution

The 33% Revolution
eMAIL DIRECTORIES TO THE PEOPLE IN WASHINGTON DC WHO CAN FIX THIS PROBLEM...

The White House - comments@whitehouse.gov

House -
http://www.house.gov/house/MemberWWW_by_State.shtml

Senate -
http://www.senate.gov/general/contact_information/senators_cfm.cfm?OrderBy=state&Sort=ASC

ATTACHEMENT "A"

If you earn	you pay %	and your employer pays %
$0 to $10,000	1	32
$10,001 to $20,000	2	31
$20,001 to $30,000	3	30
$30,001 to $40,000	4	29
$40,001 to $50,000	5	28
$50,001 to $60,000	6	27
$60,001 to $70,000	7	26
$70,001 to $80,000	8	25
$80,001 to $90,000	9	24
$90,001 to $100,000	10	23
$100.001 to $110,000	11	22
$110,001 to $120,000	12	21
$120,001 to $130,000	13	20
$130,001 to $140,000	14	19
$140,001 to $150,000	15	18
$150,001 to $160,000	16	17
$160,001 to $170,000	17	16
$170,001 to $180,000	18	15
$180,001 to $190,000	19	14
$190,001 to $200,000	20	13
$200,001 to $210,000	21	12
$210,001 to $220,000	22	11
$220,001 to $230,000	23	10
$230,001 to $240,000	24	9
$240,001 to $250,000	25	8
$250,001 to $260,000	26	7
$260,001 to $270,000	27	6
$270,001 to $280,000	28	5
$280,001 to $290,000	29	4
$290,001 to $300,000	30	3
$300,001 to $310,000	31	2
$310,001 to $320,000	32	1
$320,001 or more	33	0